At camp

We went on a camping trip. We picked the best spot right by the river.

Nat, Sam and I got started on putting up our tent.

Then we pumped up our airbeds. Nat said to Mum, "Did you bring some sheets?"

Mum said, "No, I forgot them. You have sleeping bags. They will do."

We got into our tent. Sam said to Dad, "Can we have your laptop to look up camping tips?"

Dad winked at Mum and said, "Oops! I think I forgot that." Sam groaned.

I said to Mum, "Can we have a fan in our tent? It's so hot in there."

Mum grinned and said, "I think I forgot the fan too. Let's go for a swim to cool down."

We ran to the river. There was a swing hanging off a tree.

We had fun jumping into the river and floating on our backs.

Nat said, "Can we have burgers for dinner?"
"Forget burgers!" said Dad.

He pointed to the river and said, "Let's go fishing and get some dinner."

That night, the three of us sat on a log. We had sticks in our hands.

I said to Mum and Dad, "I bet you forgot to pack the marshmall..."

"Oh!" said Mum. "That is one thing we did not forget!" Nat clapped and we yelled!

Words to blend

camp	camping	best
spot	tent	pumped
bring	grinned	swim
swing	jumping	sticks
hands	clapped	sheets
burgers	laptop	forget
river	winked	hanging

Before reading

Synopsis: Dan tells the story of when he, Sam and Nat and their parents went on a camping trip. But Mum and Dad had forgotten a lot of the things the children wanted.

Review graphemes/phonemes: ar ee oa oi

Story discussion: Look at the cover and read the title together. Ask: *What do you think this story will be about? Have you ever been camping? What is it like?*

Link to prior learning: Display a word with adjacent consonants from the story, e.g. *three*. Ask children to put a dot under the single-letter grapheme (r) and a line under the digraphs (*th, ee*). Model, if necessary, how to sound out and blend the sounds together to read the word. Repeat with another word from the story, e.g. *pointed*, and encourage the children to sound out and blend the word independently.

Vocabulary check: airbed – a mattress that is pumped full of air

Decoding practice: Display the word *groaned*. Focus on the *ed* at the end, and remind children that in some words, these two letters make a /d/ sound at the end of the word. Sound out and blend all through the word: g-r-oa-n-d. Display the word *pumped* and ask children to practise reading it in the same way.

Tricky word practice: Display the word *all* and ask children to circle the tricky part of the word (*a*, which makes the /or/ sound). Ask children to find and read the word in the book. Practise writing and reading this word.

After reading

Apply learning: Ask: *Do you think the camping trip was spoiled because Mum and Dad forgot to bring some things? Why, or why not?*

Comprehension

• Where did the family set up camp?

• What did they do to cool down?

• What important thing did Mum and Dad **NOT** forget?

Fluency

• Pick a page that most of the group read quite easily. Ask them to reread it with pace and expression. Model how to do this if necessary.

• Turn to pages 12 and 13. In pairs, children could read the conversation between Nat and Dad, making it sound as natural as possible.

• Practise reading the words on page 17.

Tricky words review

you	by	putting
said	no	do
into	your	there
was	of	oh
one	so	our